D1741539

SCIENCE DISCOVERY

SOUND AND MUSIC

Alan Ward

Franklin Watts

London • New York • Sydney • Toronto

© 1992 Franklin Watts

Franklin Watts
96 Leonard Street
London EC2A 4RH

Franklin Watts Inc.
95 Madison Avenue
New York, NY 10016

Franklin Watts Australia
14 Mars Road
Lane Cove
New South Wales 2066

ISBN: 0 7496 1036 0

10 9 8 7 6 5 4 3 2 1

Printed in Great Britain

A CIP catalogue record for this book
is available from the British Library

Series Editor : A. Patricia Sechi
Editor : Jane Walker
Design : Mike Snell
Illustrations : Ian Thompson
Typesetting : Spectrum, London

CONTENTS

THE SOUND OF ENERGY

Sound is energy. It is movement that you detect with your ears, and hear with your brain.

Try this simple test.

YOU NEED:

- a paper bag

Blow up the bag, then pop it. Don't do this next to someone's ears, because the noise can be felt as pain in the ear. You may produce quite a loud bang.

What has happened?

The exploding bag produced a wave of air that was squashed, or compressed. The wave spread out all over the room. Another way to think about the wave is to imagine that it made the air in the room shake. When a part of that wave entered your ears, your nerves carried a message to your brain, where you heard the noise.

Did you know?

Energy from your hi-fi at home can damage your sense of hearing, if you play the music too loud. Even a personal stereo can be dangerous if it is played too loud.

Ask an adult to help you with this experiment. Stand the candle in the sand and place the dish in a safe place. Light the candle and stand a metre or two away from the flame.

Hold the jug or container by the handle, and point its opening towards the flame. Give the bottom of the jug or container a hard slap with your hand.

An air wave from the jug should hit the candle flame and put it out, leaving a puff of smoke. You produced a shock wave, which is similar to a sound wave. The wave had enough energy to put out the flame.

Be patient and keep trying if this experiment doesn't work at first. Perhaps the adult helping you can hit the jug or

YOU NEED:

- a large plastic jug or container, with a narrow opening (such as a large milk or fruit juice container)
- a candle
- matches
- a dish of sand

container harder than you can. Make sure you don't hurt your hand.

Making a splash

Find out what happens when you make the energy from a tuning fork pass into water.

Practise making the tuning fork ring, by hitting its side on a book and then holding it up in the air. Can you see a blur where its

prongs are moving backwards and forwards? They move as fast as the wings of a fly.

Touch the prongs while the tuning fork is ringing. Do they tickle your fingers? Now dip the ringing prongs in the water. How big a splash can you make?

YOU NEED:

- a dish of water
- a tuning fork (if you don't have one, ask your teacher if you can borrow one)

EXCITING VIBRATIONS

There is no sound without vibrations, which are tiny backwards and forwards movements that happen again and again.

You felt a vibration when you touched the ringing tuning fork earlier (pp. 4—5). Its prongs moved backwards and forwards. Watch the vibrations when you twang a rubber band. You only hear the twanging rubber and the ringing fork when they are vibrating.

Twanging a ruler

Place the ruler on the table so that one end sticks out over the edge of the table. Press down on the ruler where it touches the table, and flick the free end. Watch the ruler vibrate, and hear it twang.

You can change the twanging noise by holding down more of the ruler on the table, so that less of the ruler sticks out over the edge.

By shortening the vibrating end of the ruler, a little at a time, you can play a musical scale. Try playing a simple tune.

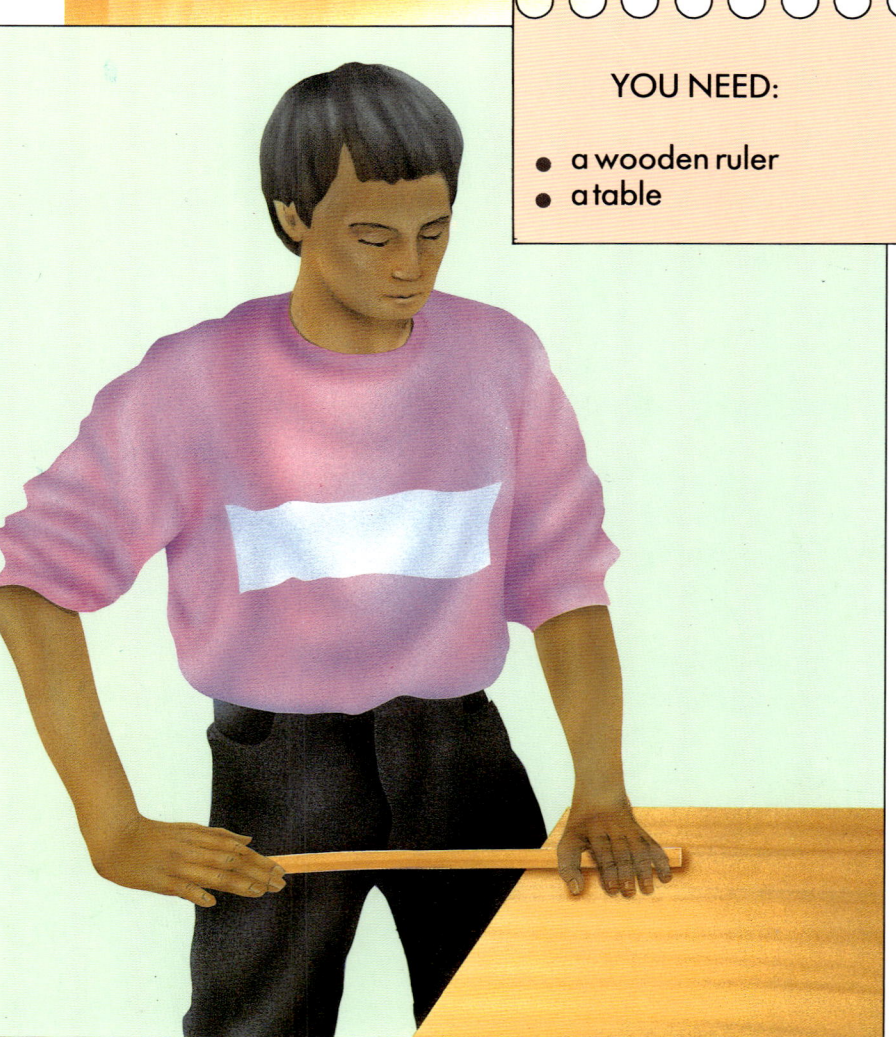

YOU NEED:

- a wooden ruler
- a table

Forceful vibrations

Switch on the radio. Tune it until you can hear music with a heavy beat. Turn up the volume control. This increases the amount of energy in the sound. If you place your hand against the loudspeakers, you will feel them vibrating.

Blow up the balloon and tie a knot in the end. Hold it between the fingertips of both hands and move it close to the radio. Can you feel the balloon picking up the vibrations from the radio?

How far away from the radio can you hold the balloon and still feel the vibrations?

YOU NEED:

- a powerful radio
- a balloon

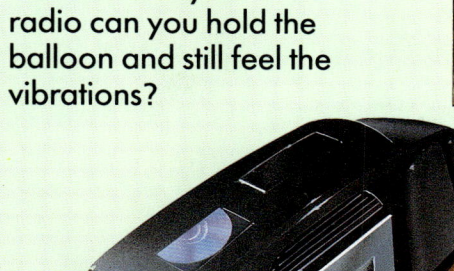

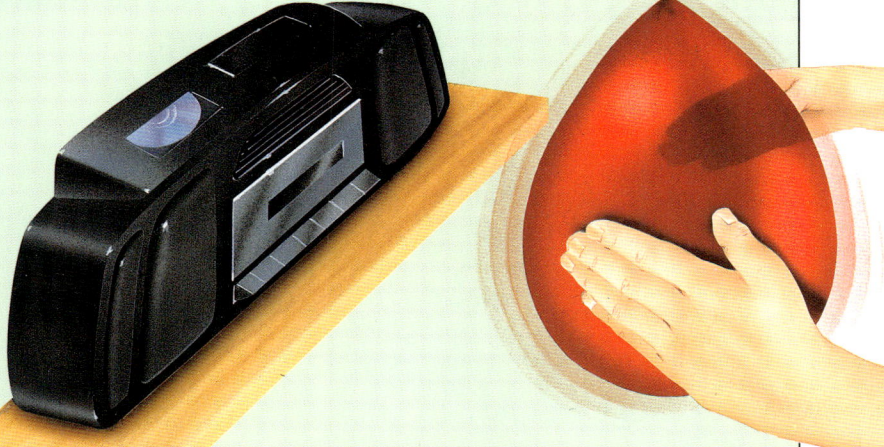

What has happened?
The loudspeakers in the radio shook backwards and forwards and sent out pressure waves of sound energy through the air. When the waves hit the balloon, they made the balloon vibrate. In a similar way, sound waves make your eardrums vibrate. Your eardrums are like tightly stretched drum skins just inside your ears.

YOU NEED:

- a short cardboard tube
- some tissue paper
- a small rubber band
- a pencil

A crazy kazoo

Stretch a strip of tissue paper between your fingers and thumbs. Hold it next to your lips. Play a tune by singing 'der' over and over again. Feel the tickle of the vibrating paper on your lips. This sounds like a kazoo, which is played in marching bands.

Use the pencil to make a hole near one end of the tube. Cover this end with tissue paper. Secure it with the rubber band.

To make music, hum 'doo' or 'der' into the open end of the tube. Try forming a kazoo band with your friends.

HOW SOUNDS 'CARRY'

Sound moves from place to place, but it needs a material to carry or transmit it. Most of the sounds you hear are transmitted through air.

A ticking clock sends out pressure waves in all directions through the air. As the waves spread out, their energy is shared with more and more air, so the sound becomes quieter and quieter.

Listening through a tube

Ask your friend to hold the clock. Move away from the friend until you cannot hear the ticking. Measure the distance between yourself and your friend.

Tape the cardboard tubes together. Stand the same distance away from the clock as you were before. Ask the friend holding the clock to help you hold the tube. Now listen for the sound of the clock through the tube. Can you hear it?

YOU NEED:

- a clock with a quiet tick or a watch
- several long cardboard tubes
- sticky tape
- a tape measure
- a friend

What has happened?
The sound waves from the clock entered the cardboard tubes. They could not spread out inside the tubes, so most of their energy was transmitted to your ear.

Did you know?
Bone is a good conductor of sound. Tap a ruler with a pencil. Now hold the ruler between your teeth and tap it again. It sounds louder the second time. The bones in your head transmit the vibrations deep into your ears. This idea is used in some kinds of hearing aid.

Can you make a sound-proof box?

When a room in your home is being decorated, have you noticed how noisy it is without curtains, cushions, sofas and rugs? The soft materials in a room help to make sounds quieter.

Put the clock in the box and see if you can make it impossible to hear the ticking sound, by wrapping the clock in the various soft materials.

YOU NEED:

- a small cardboard box
- soft materials, such as crumpled paper, cloth, cotton wool, small lumps of polystyrene
- a clock with a loud tick

Did you know?

The Moon is a silent place. There is no air to carry sounds on the Moon, but sounds can be transmitted through the ground. Astronauts exploring the Moon have to use radios to talk to each other.

SOUND WAVES

All materials are made of tiny invisible bits called atoms. When the energy of a sound wave passes through a conductor, its atoms are squashed together, or compressed. After this, they bounce apart and, for a moment, take up more space than usual.

All sound waves are made up in the same way. They consist partly of atoms being squashed, and partly of atoms bouncing apart. They are quite unlike sea waves and ripples that run across water.

YOU NEED:

- a Slinky

How to imagine sound waves

With one of your friends, stretch the Slinky along the top of a table. Give your end of the Slinky a sharp smack with your hand. (Try not to hurt yourself.) You will see a wave of energy transmitted by the Slinky's coils.

Keep smacking the Slinky and watch the waves of energy travelling through its coils. Behind the part of each wave where the coils are squashed together, you will notice a part where the coils are stretched further apart.

The Slinky shows you how vibrations of sound travel through conductors. But you must also try to imagine how the waves spread out in all directions, as they do in the air.

If you smack the Slinky really hard, the waves will bounce back when they hit the other end. They are behaving like sound waves that give off echoes.

Have you ever been up in the mountains and shouted out really loudly?

You get back a marvellous echo as the sound of your voice bounces off a nearby mountainside and echoes back to your ears.

It takes time for the sound of your voice to travel there and back. At sea level sound travels through the air at a speed of 330 metres per second.

Making another energy wave

Put five marbles in a line on a flat surface. Rest the fingers of one hand on the first four marbles. With your other hand, flick another marble so that it hits the first marble in the line. The loose marble at the far end will shoot away.

YOU NEED:

● several glass marbles

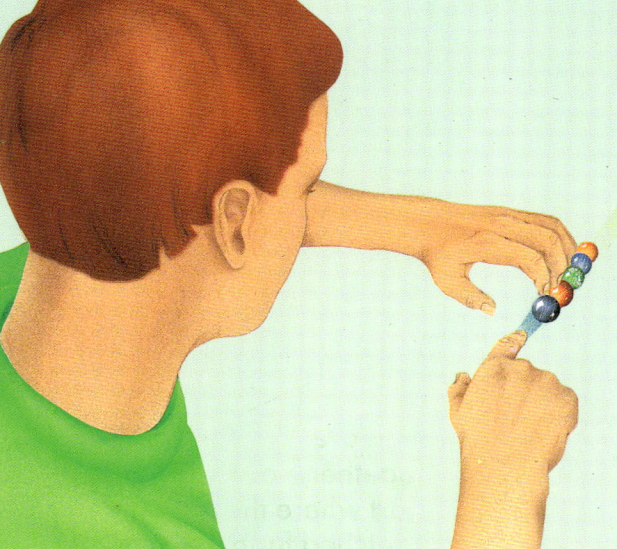

What has happened?

When the flicked marble hit the first marble in the line, a wave of energy passed from one marble to the next. This energy sent the loose marble at the end rolling away. This effect is similar to what happens in a sound wave.

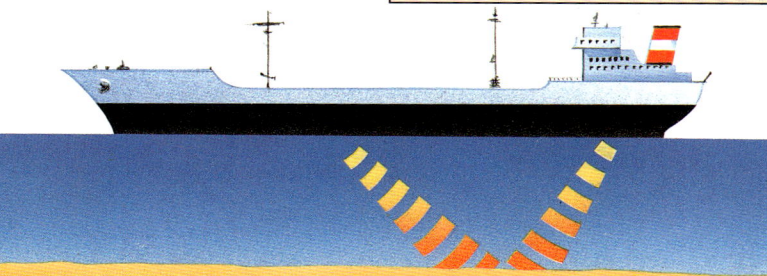

Did you know?

The time it takes for the echo of a sound signal made by a ship to travel back from the bottom of the sea can be used by ships to find the depth of the sea. Bats also use echoes to find and catch flying insects in the dark.

THE SONIC BOOM

At sea level, sound travels at a speed of 330 metres per second, or about 1,188 kilometres per hour. Higher up, where the air is thinner, sound travels more slowly.

When an aeroplane flies at the speed of sound, it has caught up with its own sound waves. As the aeroplane's speed increases, the plane squeezes them tightly and squashes them together to form a shock wave. The cone-shaped shock wave spreads out behind the plane. When part of this shock wave reaches the ground, buildings may be damaged — and you hear a loud bang.

This bang is called a sonic boom. Aircraft are not allowed to make sonic booms over land. But you may hear a much less powerful example of a sonic boom, which sounds like the 'crack' of a speeding rifle bullet.

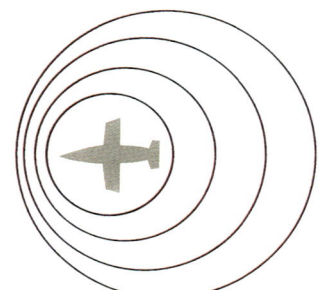
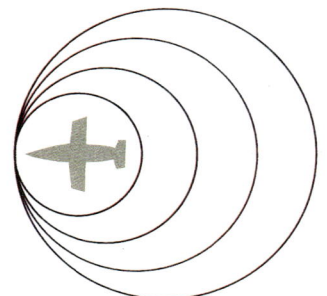
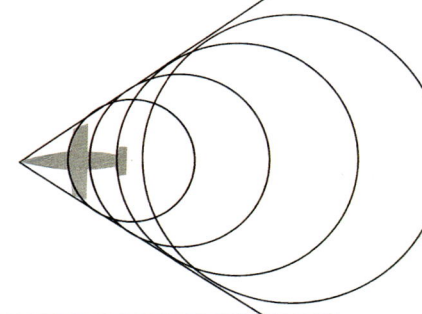

How to make a sonic 'boom'

The crack of a cowboy's whip is a miniature sonic boom. The tip of the whip travels faster than sound.

YOU NEED:

- a thin stick, about 60 cm long
- strong string
- scissors
- sticky tape

You must ask an adult to help you with this activity.

Tie a piece of string, about 1.5 metres long, to one end of the stick. Secure the string with sticky tape.

Go outdoors and find an open space that is well away from other people. Hold the stick and practise cracking the string of your whip on the ground.

You should be able to make supersonic cracks. You can feel the shock waves when they hit your ears. Soon the end of the string will become frayed. Make sure you act safely when cracking the whip.

Did you know?

The supersonic airliner Concorde crosses the Atlantic Ocean in less than 4 hours when it flies between England and the United States. It flies faster than a bullet and at twice the height of Mount Everest, the world's highest mountain. The word 'supersonic' means faster than the speed of sound.

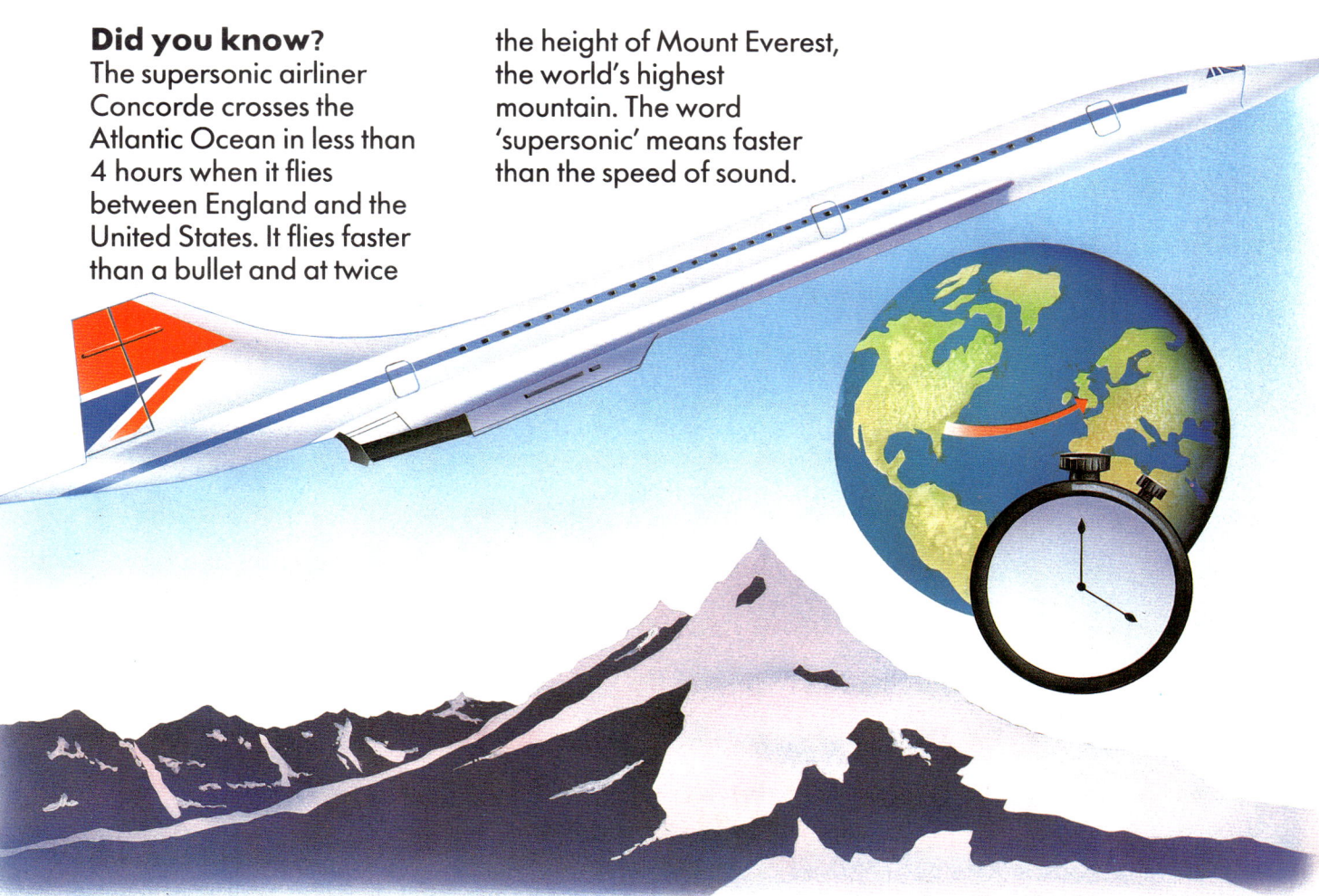

The seven 'most noisy wonders' of your world

Luckily we do not have to listen to the sonic booms made when Concorde flies over land. But we do have to put up with the sounds of other noisy wonders of the modern world.

Make a list of the seven most noisy wonders in your life. Chain saws and road drills will be included high up on many people's lists. Compare your list with those made by your friends.

Noise can damage your hearing and make you ill. What can we do to make the world a quieter place to live in?

SOUND EFFECTS FOR FUN

In theatres today, most sound effects are recorded on tape. But some sounds are still made by hand or by a machine, because they are often more effective than the recorded sounds.

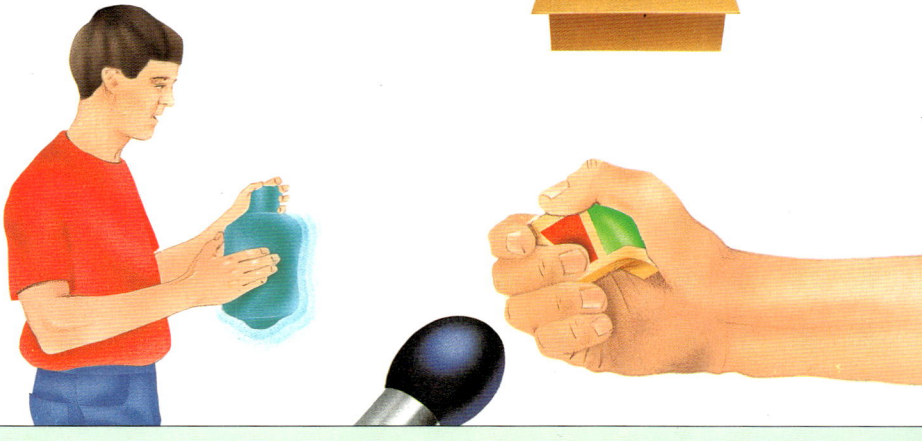

A smacked hot-water bottle sounds like a face being slapped. Broken cups and plates are tipped from one wooden 'crash box' into another, to make a dramatic smashing sound. If a wooden matchbox is crushed beside a microphone, it sounds as if the theatre is about to collapse!

Sound effects workshop

The cuckoo
Pour a little water into one milk bottle and place the two milk bottles side by side on a table. Blow across the tops of the bottles, one after the other. Notice the different sound you make when you blow across the bottle with water in.

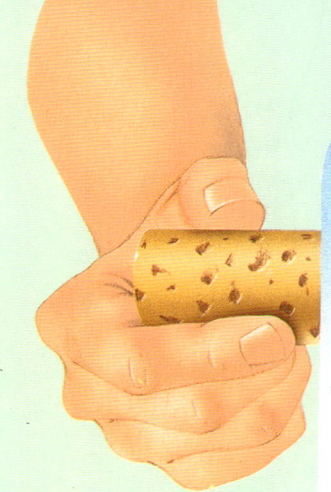

YOU NEED:

- two milk bottles
- water
- a cork
- two yoghurt pots
- a metal tray
- a bowl
- a mug

Twittering birds
Wet the outside of a milk bottle and rub it with the cork.

Disguise your voice

Pinch your nose or tap your Adam's apple while you talk.

Tape your voice and then play it back. You can hold a funny conversation with yourself.

Stuff your cheeks full of cotton wool. Telephone your friends ... and keep them guessing.

Did you know?

Special fireworks let off inside dustbins can be used in a theatre to make the sounds of firing cannons. A leather cushion whacked with a bamboo cane sounds like a pistol shot. Some old theatres had a 'thunder run', which consisted of a bumpy wooden slope. Cannon balls were rolled down the slope, to copy the sound of thunder.

Horse

Hold a yoghurt pot in each hand, and knock the open ends of the pots together. Can you make your 'horse' trot, canter and gallop?

Thunder

Hold a metal tray and bang it with your hand.

A popping sound

Fill the bowl with water and hold the mug upside down over it. Lower the mug so that its open end is just beneath the surface of the water. When you pull the mug up sharply, you should hear the sound of a pop.

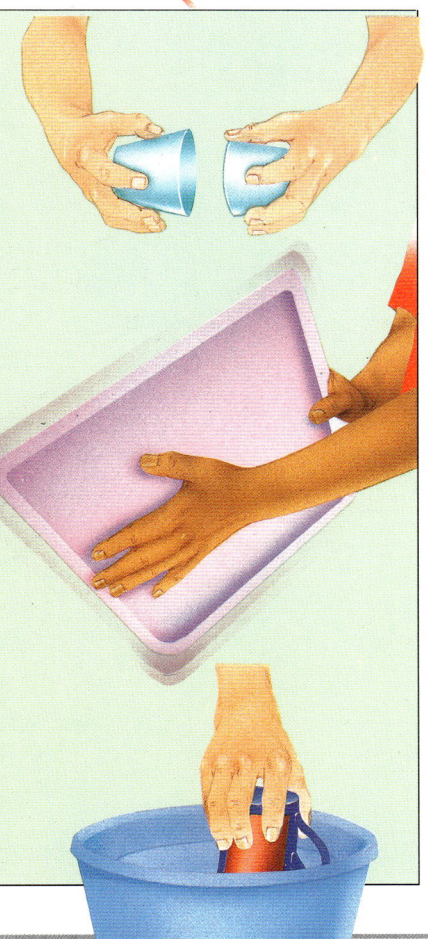

A challenge

What can you do to make these sounds?
- a dinosaur's heart beat
- the sea
- a UFO landing on Earth
- lions being fed at the zoo
- a creaking door

SOUNDS OR MUSIC?

Close your eyes and listen. What do you hear? You can hear sounds made by yourself: breathing, your heart beating, a gurgle in your stomach. You can also hear sounds in the room: wood creaking, a clock ticking, the central heating clicking. What about faraway sounds: a dog barking, a car in the street outside, the wind in the trees?

YOU NEED:

- a clipboard
- paper
- a pencil

What are your favourite sounds?

Do they include any sounds that other people find annoying? How do you decide whether a sound is pleasant or not? Although only a few people enjoy sounds that are loud or harsh, almost any sound is 'music' to someone's ears.

Likes and dislikes

Carry out a survey of the sounds that people like, and the ones that they dislike.

Ask friends, your teacher, other people in your family and at school the following two questions:
- What sound do you like best?
- What sound do you dislike most?
Write down the answers in two lists, under the headings 'Likes' and 'Dislikes'. Telephone your local radio station about your sound survey. You may get a chance to speak on the radio.

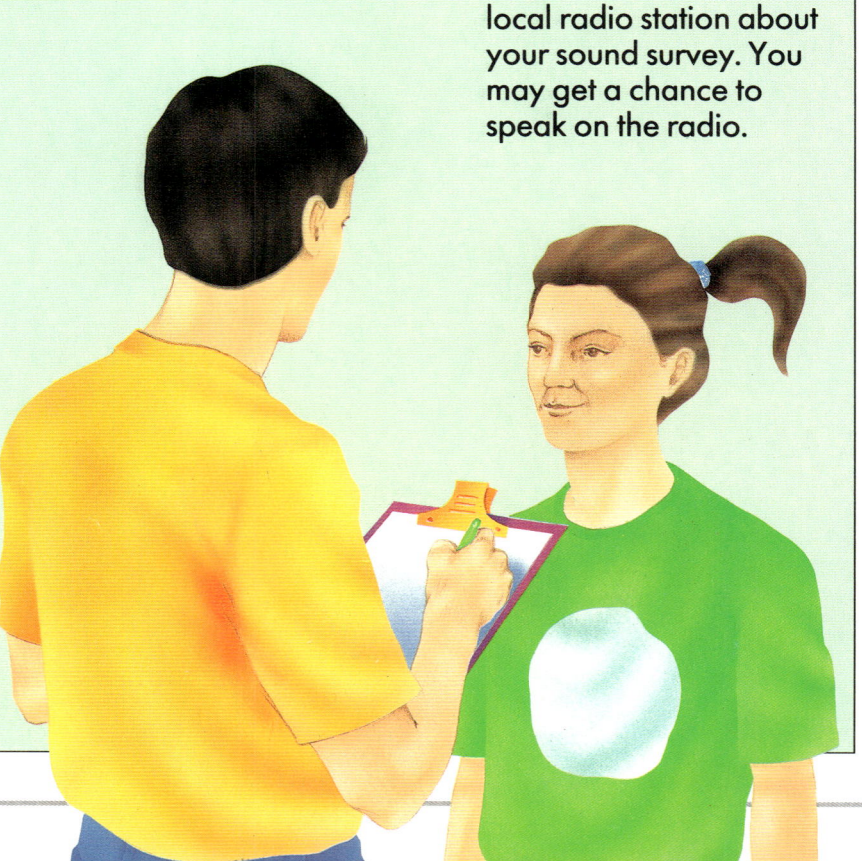

Noisy and musical sounds

Blow up the balloon. Hold it under one arm and grip the neck of the balloon between both hands. Loosen your grip to let air escape from the balloon.

As the air escapes, the rubber of the balloon vibrates and makes a sound. By pulling the

YOU NEED:

- a balloon

rubber and then letting go, you can change the sound.

People may complain that the sound is harsh and noisy. Can you make the sound more musical? You have to pull the rubber in just the right way to do this.

Weird sounds

You can make some very strange sounds with string coated with rosin, a substance that musicians rub onto their violin bows.

Ask an adult to help you make a hole in the bottom of the yoghurt pot using the hammer and nail.

Rub the string well with the rosin. Push the string through the hole in the

pot and tie a knot in the string inside the bottom of the pot.

Hold the pot lightly in one hand and grip the string tightly with the other hand. Jerk the string by pulling, but keep gripping

YOU NEED:

- a yoghurt pot
- a hammer and nail
- 1 metre of string
- rosin (from a music shop)

it tightly. As you do this, let the string slip between your fingers. You will hear some frightful noises.

Try using different-sized pots. The sounds you can make are like hens clucking, dogs barking and monsters roaring.

What has happened?

As you jerked the string and then let it slip, the rosin made it catch and then slide, again and again. The string and the pot vibrated and made the noisy sound waves.

WHAT ARE PITCH AND FREQUENCY?

The notes you produce when you press the keys on the left side of a piano keyboard are said to be 'low in pitch'. Thunder and the growling of a dog are also low-pitched sounds.

The notes produced by keys on the right side of the keyboard are higher in pitch. Female screams and the squeaking of mice are high-pitched sounds. When you sing a musical scale, you usually begin on a low note and end on a high note.

Explore the sounds you can make in your kitchen by tapping things lightly with a pencil. Try to judge whether the sounds you make are high-pitched or low-pitched.

YOU NEED:

- 8 identical empty bottles
- water
- a pencil

A bottle xylophone

Line up the bottles in a row. Fill the first bottle almost to the top with water. Tap it with the pencil, and listen to the sound. Put slightly less water in the second bottle. By putting less water in the bottle, you will hear a lower-pitched note when you tap the bottle.

Now add a different amount of water to each bottle to make your bottle

xylophone. 'Tune' the bottles so that you can play a musical scale. The pitch should change from high to low as you tap the bottles along the line. Can you play a tune on your xylophone?

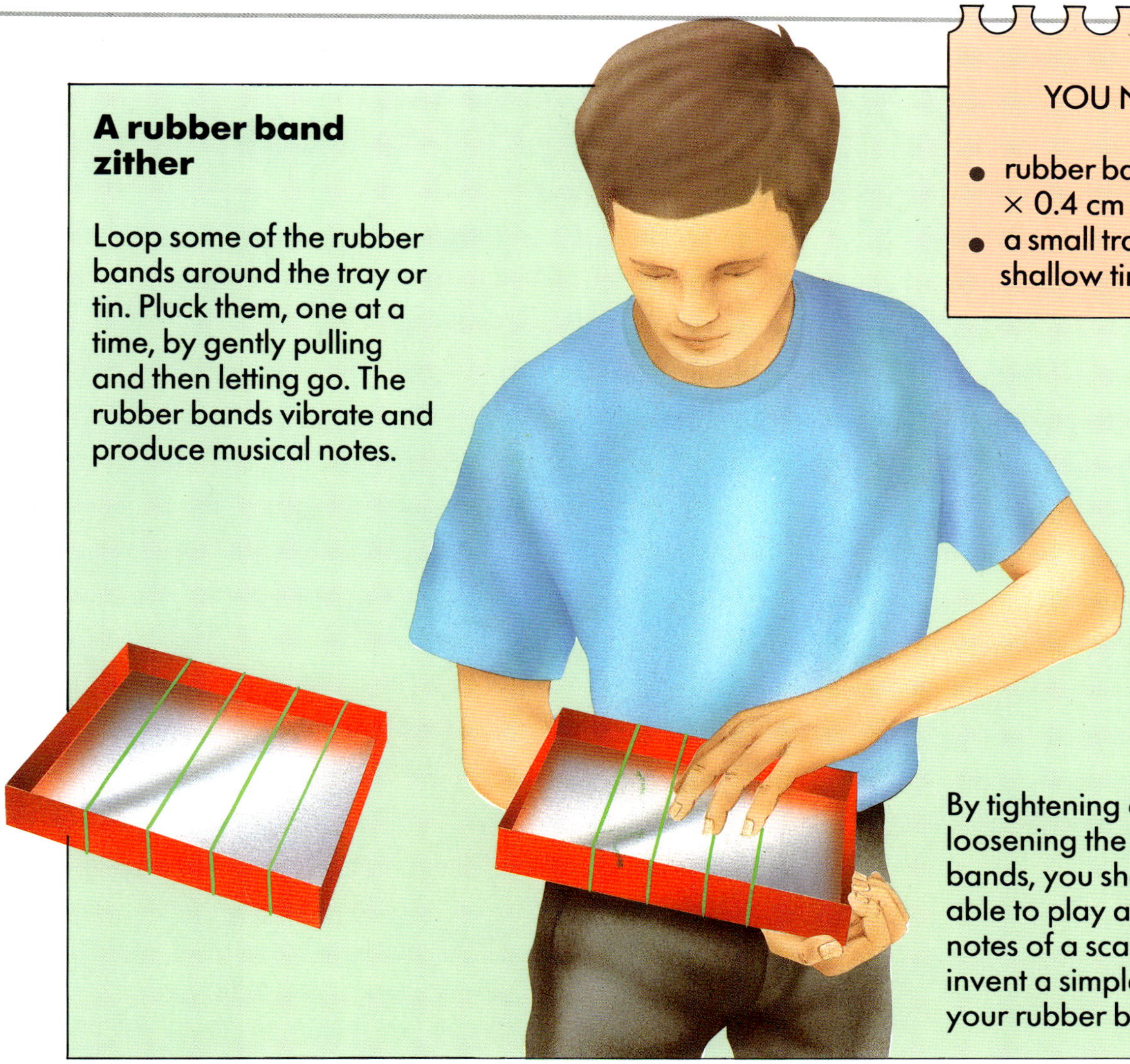

A rubber band zither

Loop some of the rubber bands around the tray or tin. Pluck them, one at a time, by gently pulling and then letting go. The rubber bands vibrate and produce musical notes.

YOU NEED:

- rubber bands (10 cm × 0.4 cm size)
- a small tray or shallow tin

By tightening or loosening the rubber bands, you should be able to play at least four notes of a scale. Try to invent a simple tune on your rubber band zither.

What is frequency?

Regular vibrations produce musical sounds. The number of vibrations that happen each second is called frequency. When you change the frequency of the vibrations, the pitch of the sound also changes.

Low-frequency vibrations produce low-frequency sound waves. You may hear these sound waves as low-pitched sounds. High-frequency vibrations produce sound waves that you hear as high-pitched sounds.

When you twanged the ruler earlier (see pp. 6—7), the end of the ruler vibrated. When the ruler vibrated quickly, it produced a high-pitched note. The compression waves it made in the air were close together and had a high frequency. The sounds made by the ruler all travelled at the same speed, whatever their frequency. They spread out in all directions.

When most of the ruler was held down on the table, the pitch was higher. When most of the ruler stuck out over the edge of the table, the pitch was lower. The shorter the length of the vibrating part of the ruler, the higher was the pitch of the twanging sound.

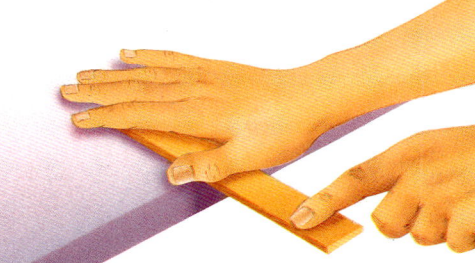

19

MAKING SOUNDS LOUDER

Microphones and loudspeakers make sounds louder. They use electricity to boost the energy of sound waves. But there are simpler ways of making sounds louder, without needing extra energy. One way is to use a megaphone.

Make your own megaphone

Form the sheet of card into a large cone, with a hole for a mouthpiece at the narrow end of the cone. Use the sticky tape to fix the cone and stop it from unrolling.

Ask a friend to stand about 15 metres away from you. Talk to your friend in your normal voice, then talk through your card megaphone. Your friend should agree that your voice sounds louder through the megaphone.

YOU NEED:

- a sheet of thin card
- sticky tape
- a friend

What has happened?

At first, the energy from the sound of your voice spread out in all directions. When you used the megaphone, you sent most of this energy in one direction, so your voice sounded more powerful and carried further.

Did you know?

A device that makes sounds louder is called an amplifier. Before electrical amplifiers were invented, people used megaphones to make their voices carry. Sailors used megaphones to make their voices carry from one ship to another.

A paper amplifier

Ask an adult to help you with this activity.

Form the paper into a cone and fix it together with sticky tape. Push the pin through the point of the cone.

Ask an adult to put an old record on the turntable. While the record is turning round, hold the cone and let the point of the pin rest in the groove of the record. You should hear sounds coming from the record.

YOU NEED:

- a sheet of paper, about 20 cm × 30 cm
- sticky tape
- a strong sewing pin
- an old, unwanted record
- a record turntable

What has happened?

The wavy groove on the record made the pin vibrate. In fact, the whole paper cone vibrated. The vibrating cone, which was in contact with a lot of air, carried the amplified sounds to your ears.

A comb amplifier

Stroke the teeth of the comb to make a crick-crick-cricking sound. Push one end of the comb against a window while you stroke the teeth again. The noise will sound louder.

Try the same test on a table, against a door, and on an upturned bowl and a wooden box. How do the sounds vary?

What has happened?

The surfaces of the objects you tested were forced to vibrate by the comb. These surfaces were in contact with a lot of air. This air also vibrated and amplified the sound made by the comb. Each surface had its own special way of vibrating, but the pitch of the sound did not seem to change. Do you agree?

YOU NEED:

- a hair comb

Did you know?

Pianos have a sounding board, which amplifies the sounds made when you play the piano. Other musical instruments, such as guitars and violins, have sounding boxes to amplify their sounds.

MAKE YOUR OWN MUSIC

Do you like rock music or classical music? Perhaps you have listened to sounds that some people said were music, but which you thought sounded like noise. It is difficult to get people to agree on what is music and what is not.

Does there always have to be a clear tune or song? Perhaps the sounds must have a regular beat or rhythm to sound like music. Music should certainly stir feelings in us, such as excitement, happiness or sadness. Maybe sometimes it should make us feel anger or readiness to fight.

What sorts of music do you like? Can you decide exactly why you like this music?

Get together with a group of friends and explore musical sounds made with everyday objects. In this book, there have already been some helpful ideas

about making music (see pp. 14–15 and 16–17). Other ideas have included the kazoo (see pp. 6–7) and the bottle xylophone (see pp. 18–19).

Here are some more suggestions for making your own music.

Scrapers

Wrap a sheet of sandpaper around each block of wood, leaving the back of the blocks bare. Use drawing pins to secure the sandpaper along the sides of the blocks. Glue a cotton reel onto the back of each block, to make a handle.

Now rub your sandpaper block scrapers against each other.

YOU NEED:

- two cotton reels
- glue
- two small blocks of wood
- drawing pins
- two sheets of coarse sandpaper

Shakers

Ask an adult to make a hole in each tin lid using the hammer and nail.

Tie a knot in one end of the string and thread the lids onto the string. Tie the other end of the string around the top of the stick. If necessary, use sticky tape to hold the string in place.

YOU NEED:

- a stick
- tin lids (use the lids from cocoa tins, baking powder tins and similar)
- string
- scissors
- sticky tape
- a hammer and nail
- a coathanger
- round bells

Use string and the loops on the bells to tie the bells onto the bottom of the coathanger.

What kinds of sounds can you make with your two shakers?

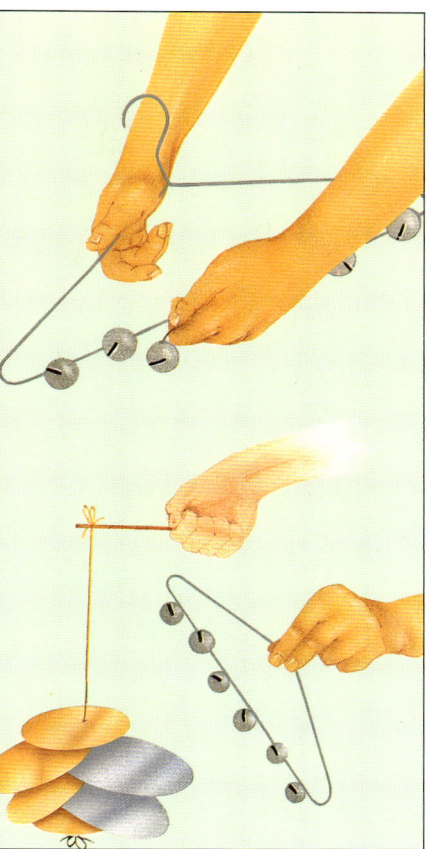

A double bass

Ask an adult to make a hole in the centre of the bottom of the bucket, using the hammer and nail.

Turn the bucket upside down and thread the string through the bottom. Tie a knot in the end of the string inside the bucket. Tie the free end of string to the end of the stick. Use sticky tape to hold the string in place.

Put one foot on the upturned bucket and hold the stick in one hand, resting its bottom on the upturned bucket. Push the stick slightly away from your foot until the string is fairly tight. You are now ready to play your double bass!

YOU NEED:

- a bucket
- a long stick (an old broom handle would be suitable)
- thick string
- sticky tape
- a hammer and nail

YOU NEED:

- about 8 wooden lolly sticks
- a piece of wood, about 24 cm × 6 cm × 2 cm
- a metal clamp (available from hardware and do-it-yourself shops)

Lolly stick piano

Arrange the lolly sticks in a line along the edge of a table. The first stick should jut out a little over the table edge. Each stick should jut out a little more. When the sticks are in position, place the wood over the top of them and attach the metal clamp to hold the sticks in place.

As you did with the wooden ruler earlier (see pp. 6–7), twang the ends of the sticks to make sounds. The long sticks will make low-pitched sounds, and the short ones will make high-pitched sounds.

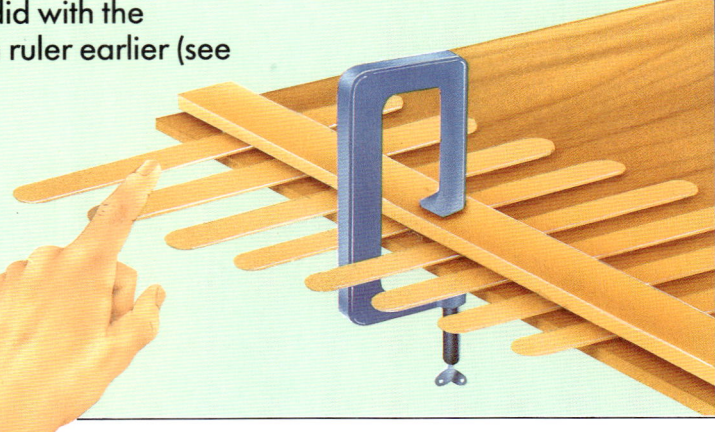

Flowerpot bells

Balance the piece of wood across the chair backs. Use the string to tie the wood to the chairs.

Tie a piece of string around one of the sticks and thread the free end through a flowerpot and the hole in its bottom. Pull the string tightly so that the stick is held against the hole inside the flowerpot. Tie the free end of string to the piece of wood.

Repeat with each flowerpot. Use the wooden spoon to play a tune on your bells.

YOU NEED:

- several old clay flower pots of different sizes
- string
- scissors
- a piece of wood, about 120 cm long (an old broom handle would be suitable)
- several small sticks
- two chairs with high backs
- a wooden spoon

Rhythm sticks

Use wooden spoons or sticks, and tap one stick against the other in a rhythm. See if you can make different sounds with short and long sticks, or thick and thin sticks.

Ask an adult to cut some notches along one stick. Run another stick up and down the notched stick to make a different sound.

Drums

Use wooden spoons or sticks to beat on drums made from old boxes or other containers. The boxes will need lids. Use boxes made from different materials — cardboard, metal, plastic — and see what different sounds you can make.

A story in sound

Make up a story that you and your friends can tell, using simple tunes, rhythms and expressive sound effects. It might be easier to hum some of the songs.

Try to include different feelings in your musical story. The music will sometimes be loud or soft, sometimes fast or slow. You could record it on tape, or perform a live concert in front of your friends and family. Make sure you practise first.

WHAT IS RESONANCE?

Everything has a natural, easy way of vibrating, which is called its natural frequency. A garden swing, if left to swing freely, will move backwards and forwards like any object vibrating with its natural frequency. If you push the swing when it is about to swing away, the force of its vibrations increases.

When sound waves hit an object, they make it vibrate. If the sound waves hit something that has the same natural frequency, they are especially forceful.

If a sound from your hi-fi has the same natural frequency as an object in the same room, the energy from the sound will make the object buzz or ring. This effect is called resonance.

Singing strings

Ask an adult to help you. Lean over the strings of the piano and sing a loud note. The strings that make the same notes as you make will resonate. They vibrate in response to your voice.

YOU NEED:

- a piano, with its strings showing

What has happened?
The sound waves from your voice had the same natural freqency as the piano strings, so they forced the piano strings to vibrate. If you had pressed the piano's loud pedal, the strings would have continued singing after you stopped.

Resonating bottle

Blow across the rim of one bottle, to make a musical note. At the same time, hold the mouth of the other bottle next to your ear. The note also sounds in the second bottle.

Sound waves from the air in the first bottle made the second bottle resonate and vibrate in the same way, so that it gave the same note.

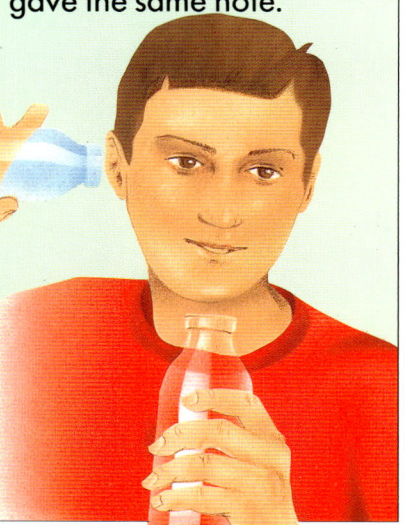

YOU NEED:

- two identical glass milk bottles

Did you know?

Opera singers claim that they can smash glasses with their sound waves. If they sing pure notes, with great force, at glasses that have the same natural frequency as the notes, the glasses are said to shatter.

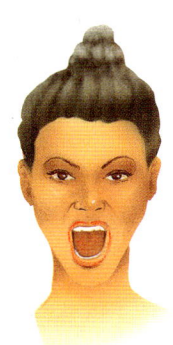
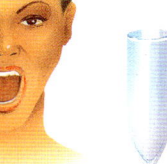

YOU NEED:

- two glasses
- soap
- water
- a plastic drinking straw

Forceful vibrations

Wash the glasses and your hands in soap and water. Rinse off the soap and put some clean water into both glasses.

Wet one finger with clean water and rub it around the rim of one glass. Make it ring with a beautiful musical tone.

By adding or pouring out water, tune the second glass so that it makes the same sound when rubbed.

Stand the glasses close together. Slant the straw across the top of one glass. Rub the other glass to make the ringing sound. The straw falls down.

What has happened?

You tuned the goblets so that they both had the same natural frequency. Sound waves from the first glass travelled through the air and made the second glass vibrate — by resonance. The vibrations shook off the straw.

EXTRA PROJECTS

A tin 'tick-tock' to time seconds

Ask an adult to make a hole in the bottom of the tin using the hammer and nail. Turn the tin upside down and thread the string down through the hole. Knot the end of the string to stop it going right through the hole.

Tie the bead on the string where it will hit the edge of the tin when the string is swung. Tie the cotton reel to the bottom end of the string. The string should measure one metre between the hole in the bottom of the tin and the middle of the cotton reel.

YOU NEED:

- just over one metre of string
- tape measure
- cotton reel
- bead
- small tin
- hammer and nail

Let the string swing naturally. There will be an interval of one second between each 'tick' and 'tock' as the bead hits the tin. How many seconds does it take your friend to write her name ten times?

A 'magic' ringing glass

YOU NEED:

- 50 centimetres of strong thread
- a glass tumbler, with tapered sides
- a flat-sided pencil (with six sides)
- a plastic bowl
- water

Put some water in the glass. Tie one end of the thread tightly around the middle of the glass. Tie the other end tightly to the middle of the pencil.

Hold the pencil between both hands so that the glass hangs down. Make sure the glass is safely attached to the string. Let the glass dangle inside the plastic bowl. By twisting the pencil between your hands, you can make the glass ring. Don't let your friends know that you are twisting the pencil.

Tell your friends to ask the glass to count by ringing, or to answer questions by giving one ring for a 'yes' answer, and two rings for a 'no' answer. If you stare at the glass and do the trick in a dimly lit room, your friends may not see you twisting the pencil.

Tablespoon church bells

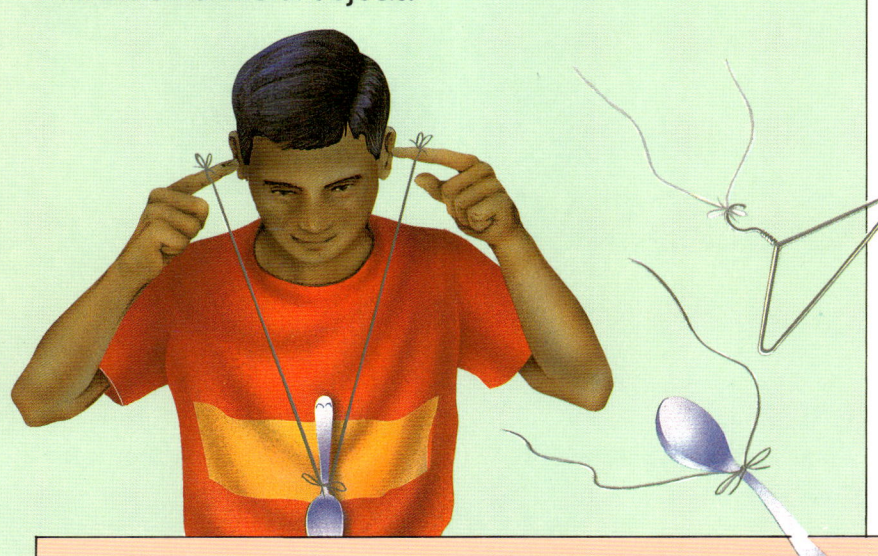

YOU NEED:

- several 1-metre lengths of string
- a metal tablespoon
- a metal coathanger
- other metal objects, such as a fork, a pair of scissors, a metal ruler, an iron poker, etc.

Tie finger loops at each end of the lengths of string. Knot the middle of one string around the spoon. Push your forefingers through the finger loops and then put your fingers in your ears. Listen while you let the spoon swing and hit the edge of a table.

You will hear a rich booming tone, like a church bell. Do the same with the other metal objects.

Perhaps the poker will sound like the famous London bell, Big Ben.

What has happened? Objects vibrate strongly at their natural frequencies. They also vibrate at the same time at higher frequencies. Normally, the higher frequencies, or harmonics, are too weak to be heard. By using the string to carry all the vibrations directly to your ears, you heard a rich mixture of vibrations.

What has happened? As you twisted the pencil, the thread caught and slipped against it, making the thread jerk and vibrate the glass. With the right amount of water in the glass, the rings will be quite loud.

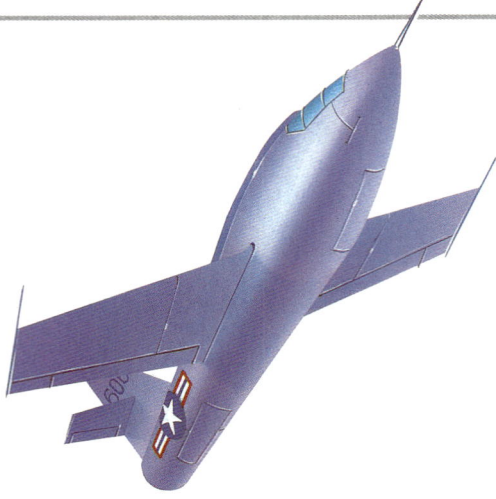

GLOSSARY

A

amplifier
Any device that makes sounds louder.

atom
One of the tiny invisible pieces found in all substances.

C

compress
To squash or squeeze.

conductor
Any material that carries sound waves.

E

eardrum
The part of your ear that detects sound waves from the air.

echo
A sound that is bounced off a surface, such as a wall or a mountain.

energy
Anything that makes something work. Energy can be seen in movement.

F

frequency
The number of vibrations per second.

H

harmonics
The weak sounds of higher frequencies that are made when an object vibrates at its natural frequency.

L

loudspeaker
A device that makes sounds louder.

M

megaphone
A cone-shaped device that makes sounds louder.

microphone
A device that changes vibrations of sound into electrical signals, to work a loudspeaker.

N

natural frequency
The easiest and strongest way that an object vibrates.

P

pitch
The highness or lowness of a sound.

pressure
The force that presses down on any surface.

R

resonance
The stronger vibrations that are produced when sound waves hit something with the same natural frequency.

rosin
A substance that is rubbed on violin bows to make them sound better.

S

shock wave
A wave of high air pressure that is produced when sound waves are squashed together.

sonic boom
A bang that you hear when a shock wave from a supersonic aircraft reaches your ears.

supersonic
Travelling faster than sound waves.

T

transmit
To carry from place to place.

V

vibration
A backwards and forwards or up and down movement that is repeated.

volume
The loudness or softness of a sound. Another word for volume is amplitude.

W

wave
The way that energy is transmitted.

INDEX